Life Resolutions

30 Days of Affirmations for an Intuitive Understanding and Empowerment

My Introduction to Love

It has been a long time coming for me to get to this point. I look back on my life and my eyes begin to fill because throughout the hardships I see a life of love and laughter. My only desire is to share this vision with my daughters. I've always wanted to live a life worthy of my title of motherhood. I wanted to be a true leading lady for my daughters to design their life after. Of course, I wasn't born with this knowledge. It was through trial, error and a lifetime of guidance that I have become as appreciative of the moments of life. I'm actually able to live and experience life instead of me running through it. I decided to sit down and begin to figure out what I could hand off to my daughters as they reach the "coming of age" point. I could always fine some authentic jewelry, clothing, shoes or housewares that could provide a visual statement as well as hold sentimental value. The longer I thought on this matter the sooner I realized that they deserved something more. They deserved something that could be taken with them throughout life. Something they would not need to repair or remember to maintain it in order for it to retain its beauty. They deserved the power that words can bring to you regardless of the era, pain, love or irregularities life can bring. They deserved the very best emotions and guidance that I could give. They deserved my heart. Even though pages can tear and ink can fade away, once read and retained these words will not only be permanently stamped in their hearts but in their minds as well.

At one time the thought of venturing into writing seemed daunting and there were not enough self-publish books or friendly faces to guide you. I had to decide what I wanted to say and how I wanted to express this all on my own. The realization is that I never needed the books. I never needed the friendly faces to guide me. After all, there was no manual on parenting but I had succeeded in getting the job done so far. Everything I needed was already with me. All I needed was to close my eyes, take a deep breath and write what my spirit told me to say. The words were not my own verbally. They originated in a place that I always knew was there but was too controlling to relinquish to. This was a battle fought for so long in my life. I never understood that to have order and control in your life, you would need to relinquish control and be guided by a force much greater than you.

This origination point is the center of spiritual restoration and guidance. I have always had these feelings and always thought of speaking them one day. However, I was compelled to see the value of printing them. Not just for my family but for anyone that may need the same guidance regardless of the age or moment they are experiencing in life.

I would like to share the importance of pursing your "self" and not the "self" others want you to be. Determine who you are or what it is that excites you beyond measure. This excitement has to extend beyond a certain salary and beyond a certain status. This excitement has to extend to PASSION. It was only through persistence and complete dedication to understanding and building a relationship with "self" and my abilities that my dream has become a reality. I still have a lot to learn about "self" that I know my journey is far from over. I have taken a vow to remain a student to learning myself and that once completed I will have achieved the life I desired for my daughters to pursue. I hope this book brings insight and assistance in your journey to making your dreams more of a reality.

Life Resolutions are the resolve for all things inhibiting success and progressive growth in life. This volume was created to instill understanding and empowerment into the lives of the readers. This was never intended to offset your original daily devotionals but to coincide with what you currently have and provoke an initiative to garner success through your own abilities. New Year's resolutions are a thing of the past. We now commit to changes that will be Life Resolutions.

This book is a compilation of two things: my desire for people everywhere to rise up and live a life resolving all strongholds and for everyone to make a point to do something positive for everyday that they have left to live. The beauty of time is that it instills all, heals all and reveals all in each of us. I am only a messenger of positiveness and empowerment. Each day provides a message that was shared through me to initiate an empowered response in life. I have fully enjoyed reading the messages for each day and I am sure you will too.

Life Resolutions: 30 Days of Affirmations for an Intuitive Understanding and Empowerment

ISBN 978-0-578-10367-9

Cover photo by BJ Graphics

Please visit us at www.aprilsheris.com and on our Facebook and Twitter networks.

Volume I

"You are not yet a Man or Woman until you understand Agape Love and implement it."

Agape love is a greater level of love that requires an infinite amount of respect, loyalty, mercy and grace for someone over oneself. Though man may never achieve such a level of commitment in the heart, it still is a standard of love that should be the optimum goal for relationships. Any type of relationship requires dedication and loyalty for it to survive. You enter into an agreement that the needs of the other person will take precedence over yours at all times wholeheartedly. This is a deeper level of maturity that asks selflessness as a standard commitment. Age has a number and of course wisdom does not. Regardless of what the mind tells the soul in respect of maturity, the ultimate gauge of weather you have lived through your immature wonderment is when you can love those you know as well as the ones you may have never laid eyes upon with Agape love.

"We are defined by the people we associate ourselves with on a daily basis. If you surround yourself with good or great people it just might rub off on you."

We are enamored with those around us as momentum to consistently be who we claim ourselves to be. Your circle will become a life source for all your achievements and sometimes your mistakes. Even though some mistakes may be inevitable, you want a support team around you to lift you from the rubble, dust you off and remind you that even the greatest people in history have fallen short of glory at times but got up and pressed forward anyway. This rally of people is a testament to the world of your level of standards for people you associate yourself with as well as expectations for self. The type of people you let in will tell a story of the level of success you identify yourself with. Successful people are aware that negativity can drag them down to a lower level of living and keep you there. Whatever you determine in your life is the peak of success, remember that your circle of support could make or break you getting there.

"Age doesn't make you wise...it makes you old! Wisdom begins with knowledge!"

The funny thing about life is that most people live it to reach a number or age. They determine in their mind that they must have experienced many parts of the world before a certain age in order to earn the title as 'wise'. To a certain degree this is true. However, many wise people have never visited or experienced what lies on the other side of the globe. They are observant and reflective in their lifestyle. They recognize that all things have a beginning and an end, cause and effect. The truth is found in believing these statements. One does not have to begin a voyage to lands unknown to him in order to gain experience. Many of life's biggest challenges may be resolved the same regardless of the country you are in. Your spirit will guide and lead you to all of life's answers if you take a moment to listen. On occasion your lesson may come from others, so you must be alert and conscious of all people you encounter. On the contrary your lesson may also come from your inner spirit. Take time to be reflective and meditative for wisdom begins with knowledge.

"Be yourself! Love yourself! Express yourself! Only then will you attract someone on the same page."

Life is unique in that it draws similarities of ourselves to us. The uniqueness is that many people believe in the old adage that 'opposites attract'. Think for a moment and realize that almost everyone and everything you have ever encountered in life had similar problems, similar likeness, similar weakness and so on. These people were mirrors reflective of circumstances you have yet to face. If you have a problem with the people that you seem to draw to you then you must change your own insufficiencies. The key to happiness is acceptance and value of self. The problem is not with the other person as much as it is with you. Correct the things that you can change in your life, then accept the things that you cannot. This turn of events will empower you to throw caution to the wind and love yourself exactly the way you are. You will no longer feel compelled to imitate someone else to fit in or be accepted. You can finally live life on your own terms and attract people reflective of love and grace. This is the way life is intended to be.

"Actions speak louder than words. So stop listening and start watching."

Words roll off the tongue so beautifully sometimes that it can enchant us and cast a spell of falsehood. The mind believes that if a person said it then they must have meant it. After all, who would say something they didn't mean right? Well, I'm sorry but you must be informed that this is the truth for some people. Determine truth by a person's fruits or actions. It's difficult to live a lifestyle that doesn't agree with your beliefs. Set a goal that you will live your life through your actions and will hold others accountable by the same standard. In doing so, you will no longer be susceptible to unwarranted hurt because you trusted what was said instead of what was shown. We must set the standard and be the standard in our own lives. Secure your desires by treating yourself with the same requirements for someone dating you. You will soon realize that the only way to discover the truth in others is through their actions not necessarily their words. The key is to stop listening and start watching.

"Relationships 101: Stop chasing people who don't want to be caught. If they want to walk out, hold the door open for them."

The funny thing about love is that it can be so powerful at times that we'd rather deny the obvious just to hold on to the false hope that this person loves us back at least equally. Never allow yourself to fall victim to a belief that is not factual or truthful. The best thing you could do for yourself and them is to gracefully accept that interest is not with you, allow them to continue running away full steam ahead and make sure the door doesn't hit them on the way out. Subconsciously, we relinquish power to the other party the moment we accept fiction over truth. Just because this person was a part of your life for a moment doesn't mean they were meant to be a part of your life forever. Appreciate what the relationship cultivated in the first place and seek the lesson from their presence. Once you close the door to your runaway love, you begin to prepare yourself for the next Mr. or Mrs. Right. It may not come immediately after and you may experience a delay in your next big love affair. Rest assured that this reflective point is necessary for your comeback into the dating scene.

The longer you stay dormant spiritually, the more comfortable you get. There's purpose for every breath you take."

This is one of the most valuable lessons you could ever learn. It testifies that we all are here to serve a greater purpose than what we are currently living. There is a spiritual presence within that counsels and guides us through all the twists and turns in life. It has existed to make the journey in life as enjoyable as possible and without unnecessary heartache. We can make decisions that turn the odds against us, so it is important to have a connection and relationship with the spirit inside. Awaken your inner spirit so that you may take advantage of life while you have it and find purpose in your existence. Once you have learned the very reason why you exist on earth, the more empowered you become. You begin to walk, talk, sing, dance and love on a deeper level. This deeper level will allow you to walk with conviction and with purpose. Appreciate who you are and the mystery in who you will become. The fact that you are still here could only lead to one truth --- that there is purpose in every breath you take.

"You can't help how you feel for someone but NEVER settle for layaway love."

Love exists three fold – past, present and future. Usually love never dies and will carry on in your heart eternally if it in fact was love to begin with. There's never a moment in your life that will shock your emotions more than when you find love and love has found you. It can make you feel empowered and ready for whatever life may throw your way. Sometimes, we mistake lust for love and continue to grow a relationship that should not have been nurtured. In life you can't help how you feel for someone. You can try to ignore the emotions that are running wild in your mind and heart but sometimes it proves difficult. However, if you ever find yourself loving someone that isn't reciprocating love on their end then you must sever all ties and end all communication. You are a beautiful individual that deserves more than someone that 'likes' you a little bit or 'could' love you one day. Tomorrow is not promised to any of us and you definitely don't want to block the flow of all thing positive that should flow your way. There is no such truth in loving someone "one day". Yes, you could gain respect for a person through bonding with them but accepting someone's layaway love plan will do more harm than good.

"Never make a habit of explaining yourself to everybody you meet. Do you & they'll thank you later!"

Certain situations can arise in your life that will cause you to plead your case or explain in detail events that occurred in order to 'clear your name'. We all have been in a position where our ego has taken over and spoken on behalf of sensibility. In these instances, you should respectfully try to rectify any damage that may have been done and salvage your reputation as best you can. On the other hand, you never want to become the person that feels compelled to explain yourself for people to avoid conflict or hurt feelings. In this world, you only have one life to live and it was granted that you would live your life standing for what you believe in. Your beliefs are your standards for living and should not be traded unless it is unlawful or causing hurt to others unnecessarily. People will respect you more because you believe in something and are willing to fight for it. Once you begin to see that, you will view life more empowered and freely. You won't feel confined or shackled to your own fears of insecurity and doubt that your words are hurtful. You will learn that sometimes who you are doesn't need an explanation and not only will you be appreciative of this fact, they will thank you later as well.

"Be the love you want to receive and never let the sun go down without telling at least one person you love them!"

Our time here is so short. We live fast paced lives striving to obtain levels of achievement and this is not necessarily a bad thing. The only problem with this is that we devalue the closeness of relationships and people in our lives. We lose sight on what really matters while we're here - which is building relationships and radiating with love to light the world. While we are here we should take a moment to appreciate those who we have in our lives… make our relationships matter so that our lives may become enriched while we have an opportunity to. Everything you give off in life has a keen way of coming back to us in various forms. If things aren't quite going your way and relationships in your life seem irretrievable it could be because you are negative in spirit and attitude towards others. The only way to fix this is to change our own ways for the positive. Whatever type of love and emotions you are in search of then you should live that lifestyle day in and day out. Love eternally, love unbiased and never let the sun go down without healing any open wounds. You never know if time will permit you to mend them later.

"Don't shrink who you are because some have height complexes. Make them stretch to your level!!"

Your time here is to live a fulfilled life of love, prosperity, peace and happiness. You were created to stretch beyond your comfort zone to face life's challenges and accept what may come in order to meet these requirements. Sure, we all become scared and apprehensive about certain things and may feel in order to become blended with others we must perform on a subpar level. However, this is furthest from the truth. No one individual is worthy of you hiding your talents or shielding your strengths to please them. Your stride in life should be inspiring to those around you and ignite the same fearless passion for their journey in life. Encourage those in your circle to stretch to your level. Always remember that you are who you are to be great and fearless in your approach to life. You don't need to do any shrinking. If anything, they need to do some stretching.

"You only get one shot at life. What's your legacy?"

Today is your day of reckoning. The day you take life by the horns and determine what you want to make out of your life. Every day that has lead up to this one was a trial effort for greatness. Greatness is now calling and asking you one very important question: "What is your legacy?" The answer to this is one that will be reviewed upon your departure. This is why finding an answer and following through is important. Pursue your dreams and aspirations and never give up on them. You only have one shot to live this life and your desire should be to live it with intention. So, grab a pen, a pad and began answering the question. What you decide to do today may affect your tomorrow.

"Your life, your mind, your passion, your path....be in control of you."

Picture this: the only thing you have to worry with is you! How empowering and simple is that? You only have to be concerned with perfecting you, growing you, nurturing you, and being in control of you. Often times in life we get overwhelmed and concerned with the trials and tribulations of others that we forget about ourselves and push us to the back burner. We should be concerned with the falls of those around us; however, we also owe it to ourselves to consider our own needs and desires. On the flipside, you must not allow someone else to control you. Never confuse control and manipulation with love. It is merely insecurities that this person has never dealt with. Love yourself through any setbacks, failures, heartbreak and isolation. You deserve the best this world has to offer and if you stay the course you will receive it.

"To thine own self be true and everything else will fall in place!! This is your only chance to live your best life!"

Some roads are better off not taking. People around you can sometimes push you way off course from where you initially wanted to go. If you don't know who you are then you will never know where you're going. Take the time to develop yourself and discover your self-worth. Realizing your full potential and the impact you were intended to make in this life is pertinent to your happiness and success. You will break down barriers and dance to the beat of your own drum. Once you master this you will accept that even though everything is not in your control, the things that are meant for your greatness you will receive. Knowing this early on is your only chance to live your best life. You owe it to yourself to start the journey of self-realization and you owe it to the world.

> *"No one is perfect and the only limits are ones we create for ourselves."*

Imagine waking up each day to a world that knows no limits. You are able to set your eyes and heart on the skies and actually experience what you imagine. Now back to reality. The thought of that may seem like a fantasy but there is truth in that vision. There are no parameters on your life unless you set them. Whatever your mind can create and perceive is the only limit you have. Start putting action to your thoughts and your imagination becomes your playground. Nothing ever created for greatness has gone without imperfections. Through this process you will also meet many challenges. Do not be discouraged. In the end you will rise when the dust settles limitless with the world at your fingertips.

"Know your own worth. It's not defined by someone else."

We all go through periods of wondering what our purpose is or why we exist. I'm sure if we all had a penny for every time we have thought of this question we would definitely have a nice savings started. The only way you will ever know the answer to this is through meditation and self-reflection. Take time out of every day to practice stillness and peace in search for this answer. There is no guru or no intellectual person that can tell you what your worth is. They may have a general idea or be close in the ball park but will never know what your worth is intended to be. Everything you could ever wonder about self is found in yourself. You could spend your whole life searching for answers and wisdom to make you self-aware; however, the only truth and wisdom you seek you will have to spend major time alone with yourself. The other benefit of this is that you will walk away so much stronger than you started. The key is understanding that everything you experience in this life is a journey. A journey that we all embark on alone and we know that our defining worth will be determined by ourselves.

"You are enough as you are because the only true failure is the failure to stop trying."

Ever look at someone that fought a long time to succeed at something and just at the turning point of success they stop trying and give up. They say that they have reached their breaking point and couldn't hold on any longer. You were probably standing there looking in shock and responding in your head that they were so close to making it, if they would have just held on a little longer. Yes, we all have known or met this person. The funny thing about this is that we have all also been that person. In times of trials and tribulations your breakthrough is usually following major objection. This "test" builds endurance, patience and faith in you that you never would have received had you not gone through this journey. The outcome is a result of you either persevering through it or failing miserably. In times of upset in your life, think for a moment of the ones that gave up right before their turning point. This should give you momentum to keep on pushing.

"Every morning I see the love of my life in the mirror!! Be #SELFAPPROVED"

You are your own worst critic and your own biggest fan. Life can sometimes have us straddling that fence on whether or not we are sufficient enough, beautiful enough, friendly enough, charismatic enough and so on. This is what I call the "Yo-Yo Effect" because it keeps you in constant limbo of who you are and what you're capable of. Well, I'm here to tell you today that YOU ARE ENOUGH AS YOU ARE. Sure, we could measure ourselves against other people every day of the week to see how and where we stand; however, we put ourselves in a position of failure because we will never be sufficient in every area of life. We all have unique talents that no one else has. Some area you will prevail in and some you will not. Let all of that go. Life was never intended for you to compete against other people. Rather, life was created for you to use the gifts you were born with and cultivate them into something so unique and powerful, a plateau no one else can reach. You are your competition because you strive to outdo your last greatest effort. Look in the mirror and see that you are your only opponent. You have your own lane that you must set fire to. No one else can be a trailblazer in this lane but beautifully efficient you.

"If you want love, give it away. Karma has a way of coming back to you"

The worst thing you could do in any relationship is to hold on tight and never let it go. Your heart may tell you that this is the best solution but in actuality it is quite the opposite. Every person needs their room to grow and space to make their own decision. Holding on tightly only makes them feel suffocated and unable to make a solid decision. They will draw back and feel rushed to make a choice. Love is definitely a delicate emotion and one must tread lightly. Release your love and allow his or her heart to either lead them to you or lead them away. Karma is the one thing that works in your favor. It allows the same energy you release into life to return to you sometimes a hundred-fold. Be giving with love. If the person never returns to you or only returns in a different way than accept what destiny has allowed. You should never want something that wasn't the best or healthy for you anyway. The sooner you realize that this process works in your favor the quicker you will realize that true love will find you. This approach is not for the faint of heart. It is for the ones brave enough and strong enough to set caution to the wind and step out into the unknown challenging what may come openly and fearlessly. This is your only shot at receiving love the way it was meant to be.

"Lord, I'm available because any success without you is failure!!!"

Sometimes you can find yourself at a crossroads in life. You find that you have exhausted all resources available to you and cried every tear you could create. You find yourself lost. This period of trepidation can occur at almost any point in your life. Sometimes it comes around too often. We were not created to know all the answers. We were not created to see the total picture. We were only allowed to see partially what may come because we have a greater source to lean on. The amount of problems that life can produce and the weight of bad decisions could be too much of an undertaking for us. The more we try to prevail and off set what has occurred, the deeper the hole we dig. Know that even at our strongest we are weak in comparison to our source of strength. When you reach this point of uncertainty and you cannot find your way out it is best to let go of the wheel of life, throw our hands up, close our eyes and cry out to your source, "Lord, I'm available to you", because at the end of the day, any success without your source is failure. There is no amount of strategy we could think of to prevail in challenging circumstances. So go to your source.

"Life is temporary and LOVE is FOREVER. Live with LOVE."

We have it all wrong. We go about our business reaching goals and accumulating wealth in life for something that is temporary. People are dying every day at varying ages. Death is not primarily an "elderly" issue. Death is an "everyone" issue. You spend your whole life trying to be somebody, trying to find somebody to love, trying to encourage somebody to be more today than they were on yesterday. However, we could live our whole life achieving these feats and receive the accolades that come along with them but a life without love is really no life at all. Love is the only thing that matters at the end of the day. We all were created out of love. We search for love from others in our lives. We share the love we have inside with friends and family. Yet, we treat love as a temporary satisfaction that will eventually die and fizzle out. Love is the only thing that we know to exist before man was created and the only thing that will carry on even after man is dead and gone. Love is constant and worth so much more than anything money can buy or respect could ever garner. To possess love and share love with a person equally eager as you is a beautiful thing that outshines any silver and gold. It is the only thing that can single handedly save a person's life or keep a person holding on long enough to see a loved one before they die.

"If you're out here dating people and your "not looking" for anything, you're wasting valuable investments - time and money! Because both of them are running out!"

Dating is a funny thing. We spend most of our late twenties "playing the field" trying to figure out what type of person we want to spend the rest of our life with. Even our parents and family condone such promiscuous behavior without fully understanding the severity of what we're telling our children. There comes a point when our minds need to readjust the concept that has been implanted into our mines. Sure, hanging out and meeting friends in social scenes is fine; however, taking them home with you or insinuating a serious relationship when you are really pursuing a "good time" is a very dangerous road to be on. You never know how the other person will accept your true intentions once they finally come out. What you do in ten minutes of your life may haunt you for the rest of your life. Be mindful of what you say or what you're asking someone. Time is of the essence and the money you're spending now for that "good time" could be better invested somewhere else. So, take your time and figure out what you want your future to be like but realize that every minute wasted and every dollar spent you can't get back. In the long run you may have exhausted all your resources and never figured it out because your focus primarily was enjoying the moment.

"It's not about where you start but rather where you finish. You now have no more excuses."

In life, we all have very different pasts and beginnings. Some are beautiful stories that play out like fairytales. Some are horrible stories of dark painful pasts. We are all intertwined in this novel of life. Regardless of where you originated or the role you played in creating your story, know that the true essence of it all in life is it's all about where you finish in the end. We all wish we could go back and erase a portion of our story or rewrite a past decision. Unfortunately, this is not possible nor will it ever become an option. At this moment, stop whatever you are doing and take a minute to think about where you wish you could rewrite your story. Even if it's multiple areas write them down on paper, place it in an envelope and seal it. Take the envelope, tear it into pieces and throw each piece in the trash. That's your way of letting go of those negative past thoughts that have been holding you back and consuming mental space from productive thoughts. You now have no more excuses and may continue on with your life making each day better than the last. This part of the story is now in your hands and we are all eager to see how the story finishes.

"Some people can't stay outta their own way enough to win!"

We've all known someone like this. They have all the potential to get ahead and free themselves from their current setbacks but can't seem to get out of there way long enough to see the great turn of events. The irony of this is that each one of us has been on both sides of this fence. We have witnessed these things happening and we have been the one holding up greatness from entering into our own lives. Think about this: insanity is defined as continually doing the same thing repetitively but expecting different results every time. You cannot produce a different thought pattern, lifestyle, relationship, insight, etc. if you never jump out there and try something new! The unexpected is a scary thing. You could think of all the negative aspects that may be associated with what you have never tried but you also have some very negative aspects by staying with what you know-comfort zone. Never let your inability to try something else be the reason why your greatness has never met you. You owe it to yourself and your destiny depends on you taking a chance on something you've never experienced before. It was scary for each and every one of us that did step out on faith. So, just like you see these terrible habits in your friend and are awaiting them to take a chance on destiny, we are waiting for the same thing with you.

"You must produce positive thoughts in order to produce positive results."

Negativity seems to accommodate our mental space more so than less. It will setup and establish itself permanent residence in our minds when we are least expecting it. The only chance we have of evicting negative thoughts from our minds is to produce positive affirmations in our minds every moment of our day. Sure it is difficult to do; however, the more routine it becomes the easier it is to do. There is always going to be a sliver of positiveness in anything that comes your way in this life. It is your responsibility to seek it. Once you reprogram your thinking to always finding the "good" amidst all the bad, you will never have room for negative energy or thoughts to live in your mind. You will never be capable of producing any positive actions in your life until you begin to think positive. Declare today the day your mind is under new management. Your first order of business is to evict your old tenants of pessimism and make room for you new tenants of optimism. Once you do this the sky becomes the limit in your life.

"Enjoy the trip down memory lane and redefining who you are."

There is importance in discovering all the facets of YOU. Sometimes as parents we tend to overlook a very important teaching in child rearing. That important factor is self-discovery. We get consumed with learning everything we can in school, when travelling, in new people we meet but never ourselves. You may be choosing lovers based on areas in your life that need fulfillment. We tend to attract people that are mirrors of us and so you have two people together with the same insufficiencies trying to find fulfillment in the other. The two of you will never get anywhere because you're both depleted in those areas and so the relationship fizzles out and it's over. Try taking the time to learn everything about you. What you like to do, what you don't like, what type of people you prefer associating yourself with, what type of woman or man that works with your personality and etc. are all questions you should be trying to figure out. This is not a rush process. Don't try to hurry up through this so you can get back in another relationship. There is a woman or man out there that will match your personality and the two of you can join together to produce positiveness. The focus is to live your life doing everything you could think of doing while you are redefining 'WHO YOU ARE'. Once you are finished with this task, you will have enjoyed the trip down memory lane because everything will be clear to you in regards of your outlook.

"I know it isn't easy but nobody's perfect."

Forgiveness is one of life's toughest lessons. We are able to digest hurt, pain, loss, and failures easier than we can digest forgiveness. The idea of letting someone off the hook or releasing them from their bad decisions is difficult. However, in order to be forgiven in this life by others we must forgive people who have assaulted us. No one said it will be easy or that you can accomplish this in the blink of an eye. Just start to understand that some people have experienced a pain so deep that the best judgment they could make at that time was the option they chose. It is not to say that we could go around making bad choices and expecting forgiveness for it, but more so to understand that the origination of the hurt was from poor judgment that we all have made from time to time and the only light at the end of the tunnel came when someone had forgiven us at that time. The notion of forgiveness has the power to change a person's life. You releasing the guilt, pain and hurt from them in your life allows you to be free. They no longer will hold you captive by their assault against you or your bitter feelings toward them. Also, the idea that someone cared enough to forgive them of their misfortune may be all they needed to take a different route next time. At the end of the day we all would like to be forgiven and know that in that person's heart we have an opportunity to start anew with them. Don't be judge and jury over someone else. You never know when your neck will be on the chopping block and when you will need their saving grace.

> *"Remember that with LOVE actions speak louder than words. Only way they'll get the point."*

Think back on a time when someone told you something significant but their actions proved otherwise. For instance, how many times have someone told you they were sorry but you witness them doing the same thing over and over again. That's the strangest thing about any type of relationships. We grow up waiting on a man or woman to speak three of the most beautiful words to us never realizing that there is more power in actions. Yes, we all long to hear 'I love you' come out of the mouth of someone that means the world to us. However, it should have some pre-cursors and post-cursors to coincide with what you are waiting to hear. Love is an action word. By nature when our mind realizes that we love someone our innate instinct is to begin works that exhibit our idea. We do this often times subconsciously and it may be a while before we realize that a change has been made. Once the correlation is made between our thoughts and our actions, then we begin to confess with words our intention. This is a wonderful cycle in life that should never leave the other person guessing or wondering whether or not the words are true. You could talk to a person until you are blue in the face but often times that person is waiting on a sign or clue via your actions before believing whole heartedly. There is a lot to lose in matters of the heart. You don't want to speak something but not follow through with actions. That damages trust in what you say and makes it more difficult to re-establish that in the future.

"We all influence the lives of younger generations either directly or indirectly. So, what story are u encouraging them to live?"

I remember as a child growing up wishing I was a great super star singer. I watched young teen stars around my age and wanted to be everything they were so I can experience life they were living. The older I got, I soon realized that everything isn't for everybody. As I reflected on this not too long ago I understood the importance of the role we play in assisting to molding the lives of generations under us. I never pictured myself the role model type but in some way or form I am a role model to people younger than me that I come into contact with often. At that moment clarity struck me: I am one of many images of adulthood for them. What impact would be the best impact for me to make on them? This became my responsibility even more once I became a parent myself. We each hold an indirect or direct responsibility to younger generations. We can no longer count them out, blame their parents and society or feel anxiety about our future because of the state our youth is in. We should be projections of how they should conduct business and navigate through life once they reach our age. We can no longer say that it is out of our hands or not our responsibility. The challenge is calling for us to step up to the plate and strike a homerun for the team. It has always took a village to raise a child. Together we can impact the lives of every child created for the better. What are you waiting on?

"Most things in your life may change but there is one constant in your life.....watch the throne. #Spirituality"

Money will come and go. Friends will come and go. Jobs will come and go but there is one thing in life that we can count on to remain the same no matter which way the wind blows and that is Spirituality which equates to love. This is the totality of everything that I try to get you to understand. Without Love everything else in life will lose its color. This world that we live in was vividly painted for our inhabitance out of love for us. Every relationship in your life, weather intimate or not, holds a certain level of love at the core. Every sight you've ever admired, every person you've ever lost or every success you've ever experienced held at its core the essence of love. Do not make haste in your life believing that one can exist without love. It was encrypted into the being of every man, woman and child. Release anything in your life that is consuming you or subtracting and dividing from your life. In order for you to live to your fullest potential and encompass the love that exists for you, you must envelope yourself in people that will add to you and multiply your endeavors. This is necessary in order to occupy love in your life and share your love with others. To be in love is a beautiful thing but to radiate love is even better.

No Carbon Copy

I want you to know how precious you are.

How you were created with many scars.

But the scars do not defy your beauty.

It's more like they serve as double duty.

The way I see it is you have to decide.

Which people are worthy of you bringing inside.

Their envy, judgment and hatred is surplus.

Good thing you understand whose opinion is just.

You were created with intent.

Not a detail left out without His consent.

So view your scars as stripes you've earned.

As prideful warfare; as lessons learned.

Scars serve a purpose and tell the greatest story.

It's a snapshot of your life's journey.

They also show people how you stand with pride.

Despite the circumstances or how you almost died.

The point I want to make is to let the real you shine.

Don't worry about being ridiculed or left behind.

The ones that' re worthy to make it to the final round.

They are precious jewels in your life you've found.

They serve to uplift, celebrate and bring out your best.

Not to worry about the ones that couldn't finish the test.

See, they folded and crumbled and relinquished in fear.

Because they saw that your greatness and potential was near.

Hold true to these words for they hold the truth.

Of how valuable you are if you ever need proof.

The next time someone doesn't recognize your beauty.

Simply inform them of how scars serve double duty.

How it's okay if they want to blend in with others.

But you are an original; a Picasso or Van Gogh for starters.

It's the one's that hide and blend in that's the problem.

They can't stand the sight of themselves; so they look for faults in others like them.

They spend every waking day and night trying to understand you.

How you make life seem so sweet and happy; a life they never knew.

So wear your scars with pride and on exhibit for all to see.

Because they'll never be another like you – no carbon copy.

Your Journey

Jot down the inspiration you got from each day's message. Keeping a journal of your thoughts will help Life Resolutions be more meaningful to you.

Notes

_____
_____
_____
_____
_____
_____
_____
_____
_____
_____
_____
_____
_____
_____
_____
_____
_____
_____
_____
_____
_____
_____
_____
_____
_____
_____

Notes

_____
_____
_____
_____
_____
_____
_____
_____
_____
_____
_____
_____
_____
_____
_____
_____
_____
_____
_____
_____
_____
_____
_____
_____
_____
_____

Notes

_____

_____

_____

_____

_____

_____

_____

_____

_____

_____

_____

_____

_____

_____

_____

_____

_____

_____

_____

_____

_____

_____

_____

_____

_____

_____

Notes

_____
_____
_____
_____
_____
_____
_____
_____
_____
_____
_____
_____
_____
_____
_____
_____
_____
_____
_____
_____
_____
_____
_____
_____
_____
_____
_____
_____

Notes

_____

_____

_____

_____

_____

_____

_____

_____

_____

_____

_____

_____

_____

_____

_____

_____

_____

_____

_____

_____

_____

_____

_____

_____

Notes

_____
_____
_____
_____
_____
_____
_____
_____
_____
_____
_____
_____
_____
_____
_____
_____
_____
_____
_____
_____
_____
_____
_____
_____
_____
_____

Notes

_____
_____
_____
_____
_____
_____
_____
_____
_____
_____
_____
_____
_____
_____
_____
_____
_____
_____
_____
_____
_____
_____
_____
_____
_____
_____
_____
_____
_____

Notes

_____
_____
_____
_____
_____
_____
_____
_____
_____
_____
_____
_____
_____
_____
_____
_____
_____
_____
_____
_____
_____
_____
_____
_____
_____
_____
_____
_____

Notes

_____

_____

_____

_____

_____

_____

_____

_____

_____

_____

_____

_____

_____

_____

_____

_____

_____

_____

_____

_____

_____

_____

_____

_____

_____

_____